A WORD CONCEPT BOOK

Where is my Friend?

By Betsy and Giulio Maestro

CROWN PUBLISHERS, INC., NEW YORK

For Daniela

Text copyright © 1976 by Betsy Maestro
Illustrations copyright © 1976 by Giulio Maestro
All rights reserved. No part of this publication may be reproduced
or transmitted, in any form or by any means, electronic, mechanical,
photocopying, recording, or by any information storage
and retrieval system, without the prior written permission of the publisher.
Published by Crown Publishers, Inc., 225 Park Avenue South, New York, New York 10003
and represented in Canada by the Canadian MANDA Group
Crown is a trademark of Crown Publishers, Inc.
Manufactured in Italy
Designed by Giulio Maestro

Library of Congress Cataloging-in-Publication Data
Maestro, Betsy.
Where is my friend?
(A Word concept book)
SUMMARY: Harriet's search for her friend introduces a
number of location words.
[1. Space perception—Fiction] I. Maestro, Giulio.   II. Title.
PZ7.M267Wh   [E]   75-15902
ISBN 0-517-52436-8

10 9 8 7 6 5 4

Where is my Friend?

Harriet was looking
for her friend.

She climbed **up** a tree.

She came **down** again.

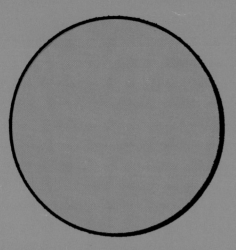

Harriet looked **between** two trees.

She walked **around** the trees.

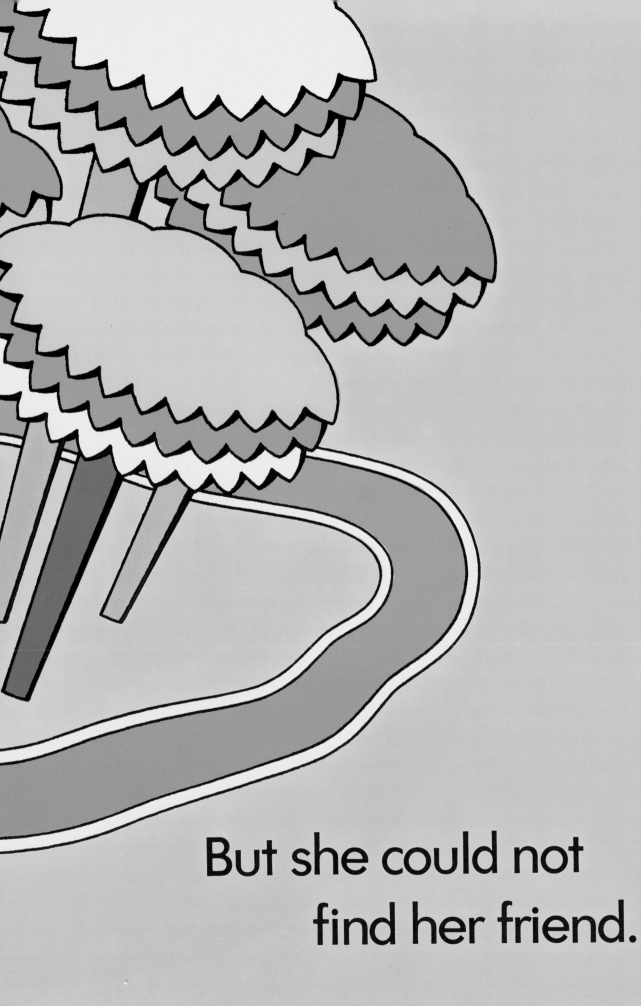

But she could not
find her friend.

So Harriet went **through** a gate.

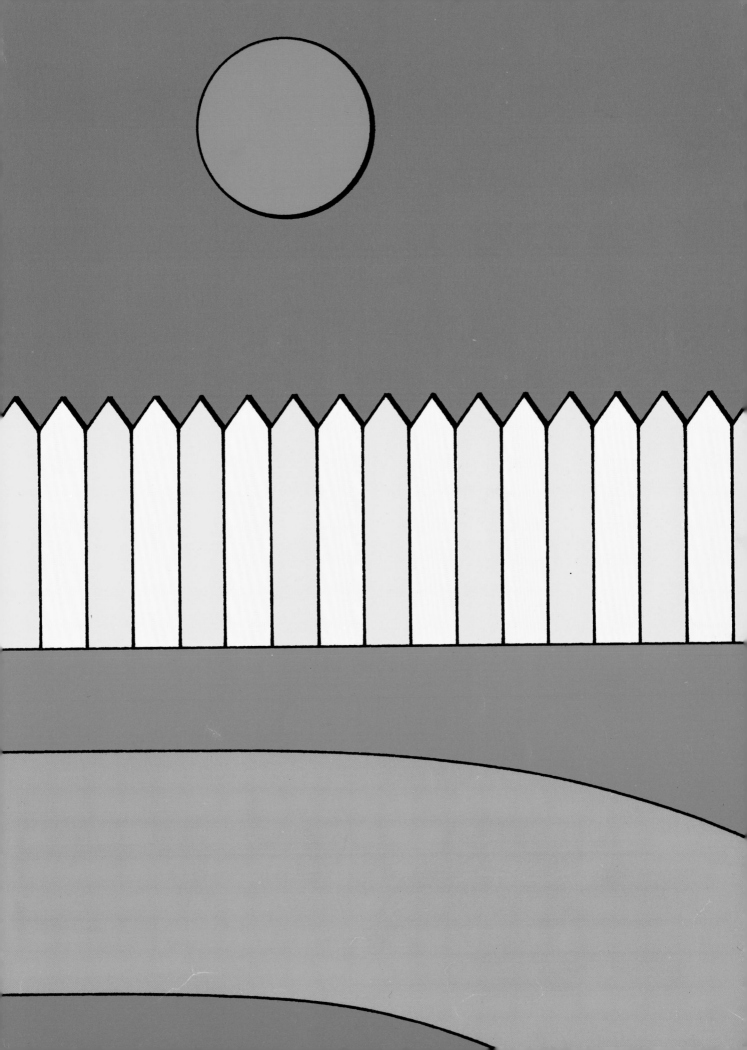

She looked **under** a rock.

She flew **over** a hill.

She went **into** a cave...

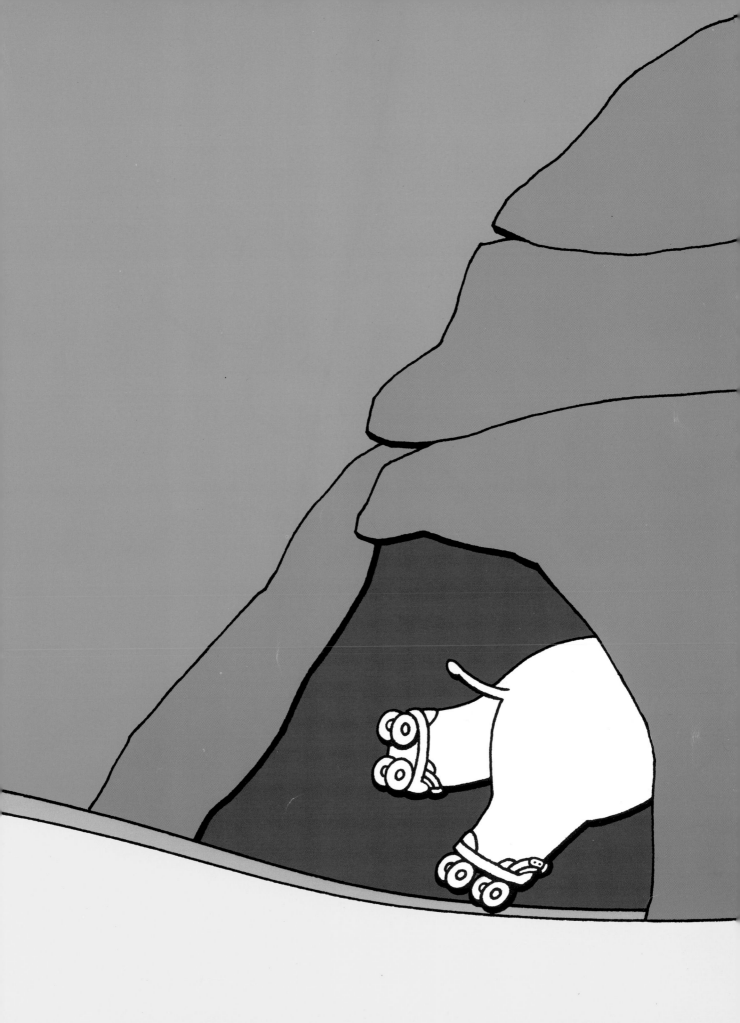

and she came **out** again.

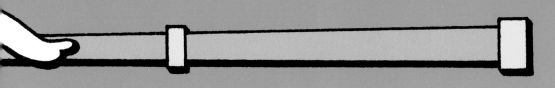

Harriet climbed **on** a chair
to look for her friend.

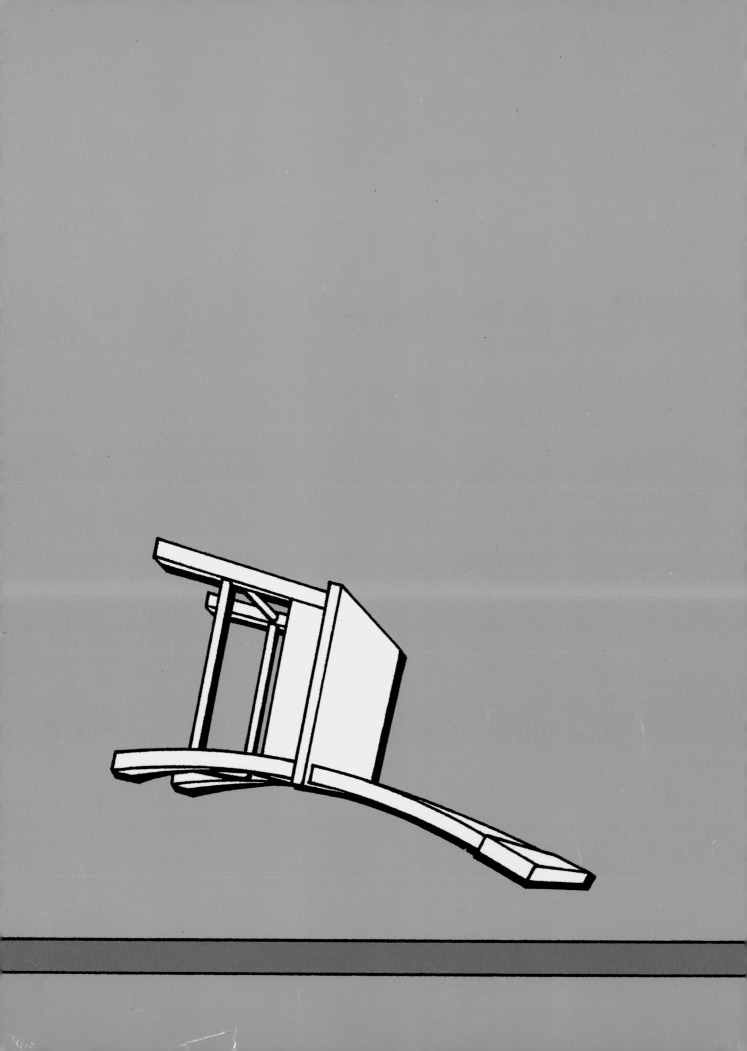

Then she got **off** again.

She looked **behind** her.
No one was there.

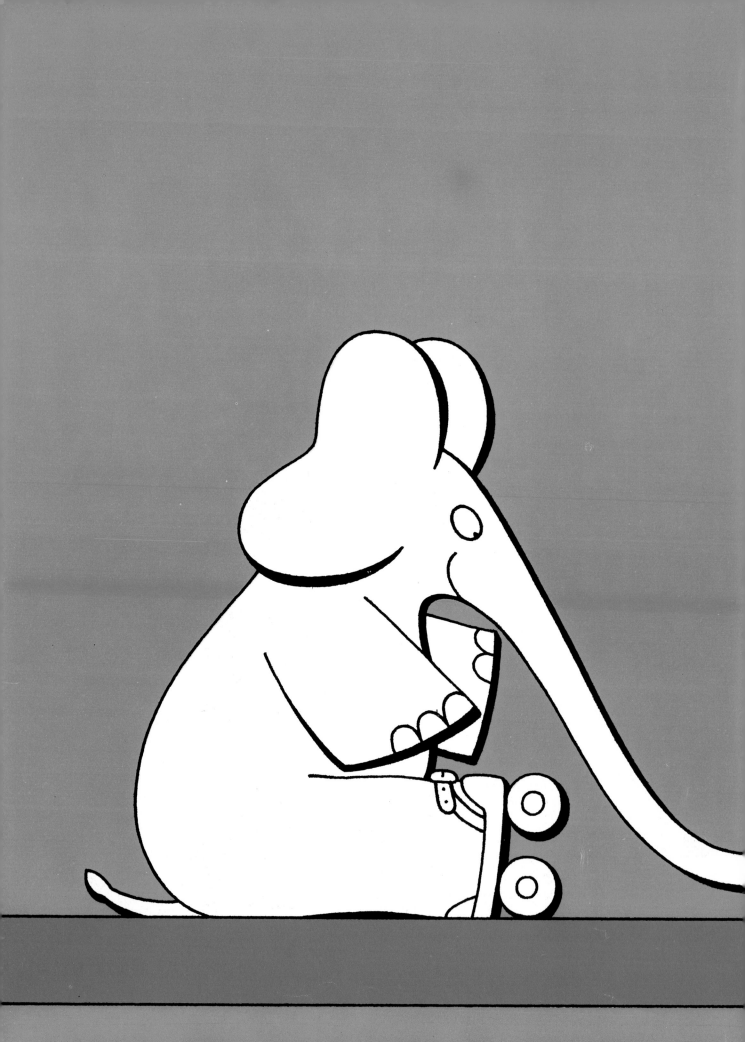

Then Harriet looked again, and there was her friend, right **in front** of her nose!

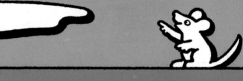

Habitats

ARCTIC TUNDRA

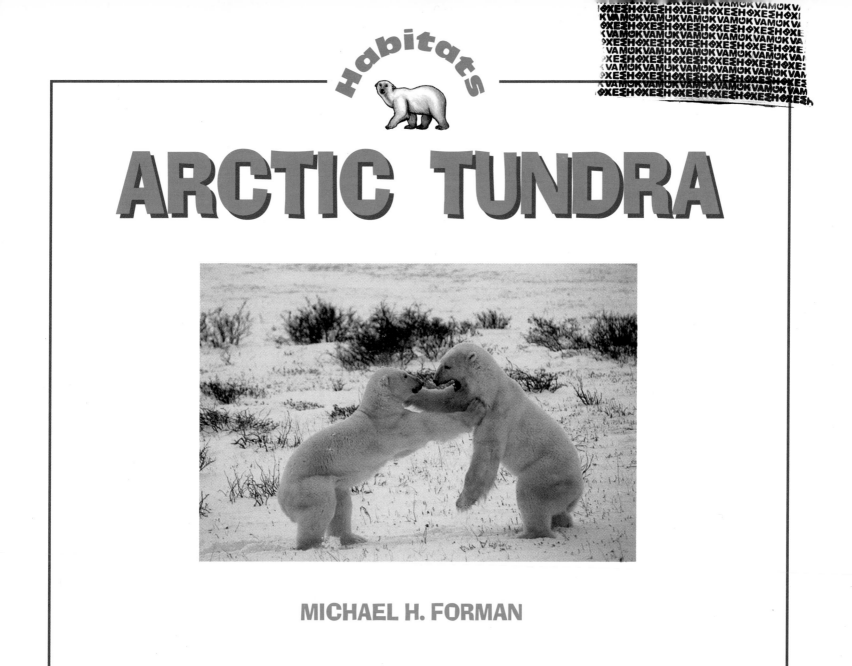

MICHAEL H. FORMAN

Ⓟ **Children's Press**

A Division of Grolier Publishing
New York London Hong Kong Sydney
Danbury, Connecticut

Created and Developed by The Learning Source

Designed by Josh Simons

Acknowledgment: We would like to thank Tom Stack of Tom Stack & Associates for his assistance with this project. His help is greatly appreciated.

All illustrations by Arthur John L'Hommedieu

Photo Credits: Anna E. Zuckerman/Tom Stack & Associates: 4–5 (background); Brian Parker/Tom Stack: 16 (left), 20; Craig Brandt: 6–7 (background), 7, 24 (left), 26, 28 (right); Jeff Foott/Tom Stack: 15; John Shaw/Tom Stack: 18 (inset) 19, 26 (background); Robin Brandt: 2–3 (background), 22, 23 (background), 25, 32; Thomas Kitchin/Tom Stack: 13; Tom & Pat Leeson: 1, 3, 4–6, 13 (left), 14, 15 (bottom), 1– 18, 23, 24 (right), 25 (right), 27, 28 (left), 29; W. Perry Conway/ Tom Stack: 8–9, 12; Warren Garst/Tom Stack: 16 (right); Wendy Shattil/Bob Rozinski/Tom Stack: 20–21.

Forman, Michael H.
Arctic tundra / by Michael H. Forman.
p. cm. -- (Habitats)
Summary: Describes the characteristics of the tundra and the plants and animals that live there.
ISBN 0-516-20710-5 (lib. bdg.) 0-516-20372-X (pbk.)
1. Natural history--Arctic regions--Juvenile literature. 2. Tundras--Juvenile literature. [1. Tundras. 2. Tundra ecology. 3. Ecology.] I. Title. II. Series: Habitats (Children's Press)
QH84.1.F65 1997
508.311'3--dc21   96-52919 CIP AC
© 1997 Children's Press®, a division of Grolier Publishing Co., Inc.
Printed in the United States of America
1 2 3 4 5 6 7 8 9 10 R 06 05 04 03 02 01 00 99 98 97

Far to the north—almost at the North Pole —is a land called the tundra. To get there, you must travel over icy waters where whales leap and walruses lie on cold, rocky shores.

You must also go beyond the thick forests of evergreens where wolves hunt and howl. Then you must cross the valleys where moose struggle through mounds of fresh, deep snow.

The tundra forms a huge ring around the very top of the world. It stretches from northern Canada to Greenland and Norway and then on to Russia and Alaska.

Finally, you would come to the strange quiet world of the tundra. For most of the year, this nearly treeless land is dark and frozen. Temperatures fall so low that water can turn to ice within moments.

Surprisingly, only small amounts of snow and rain fall on the tundra. In this way, it is very much like a desert. But unlike a desert, the tundra is one of the coldest places on earth. It is this extreme cold that controls the life of every plant and animal living here.

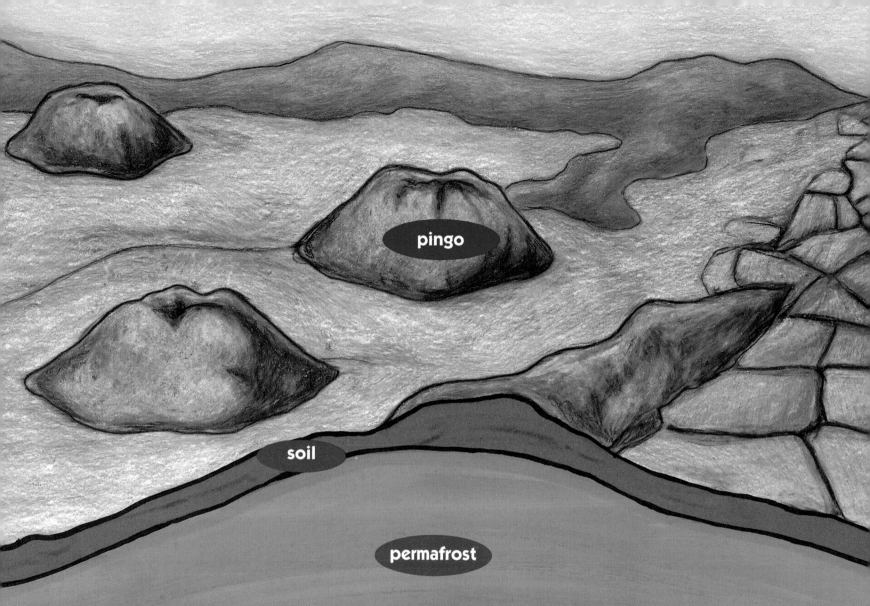

The arctic weather affects even the ground. Each year the top layer of soil freezes and thaws out. But the thick second layer, called the permafrost, never gets warm enough to thaw. So, water from the top layer isn't able to drain down into the frozen permafrost. Having nowhere to go, the trapped water does strange things to the land.

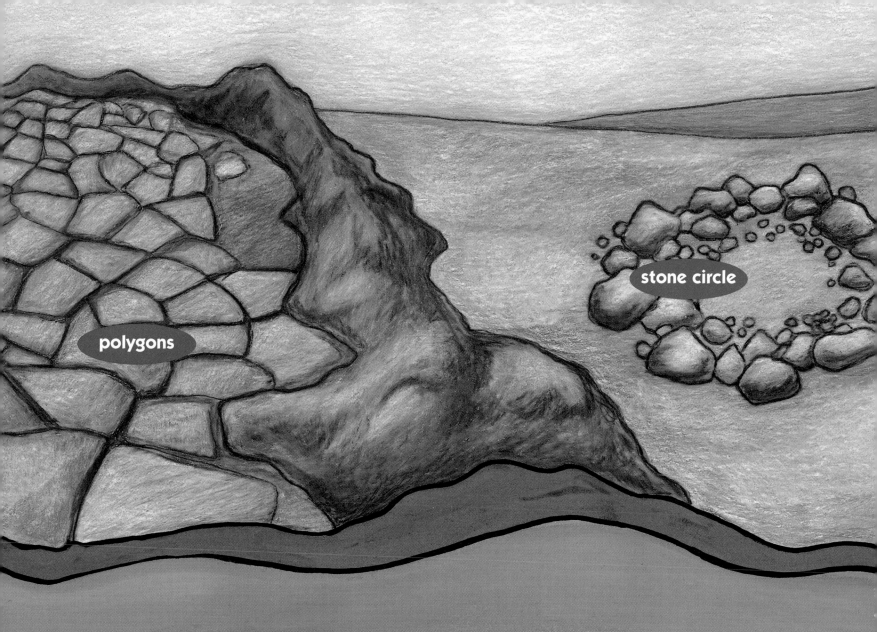

polygons

stone circle

For one, trapped pools of water often push large hills of soil, called pingos, up through the surface. Other times, the water makes unusual polygon shapes on the ground. And sometimes, the freezing water even moves rocks around, forming giant circles of stone.

For most of the year, winter rules over the tundra. During this bitterly cold time, there is either very little sunlight or none at all. From December to February, twelve o'clock noon seems more like late evening than the middle of the day.

Only the Northern Lights break through the darkness. These appear in the sky when electricity from the sun strikes the earth's atmosphere. Then the sky seems to explode with streaks of green and white and rose.

Most birds and animals must leave the tundra long before winter begins. Only those few creatures able to survive the arctic cold remain.

Chubby ptarmigans, like this one, pass the days warming themselves in any sunlight they can find. Their white winter feathers make it hard for enemies to see them against the snow. Certain insects, such as mosquitoes, have ways to keep themselves from freezing. Some drain all the water from their bodies while others build up special chemicals.

Furry arctic foxes and sleek-bodied weasels also have thick, white coats in winter. Their coats make the animals nearly invisible as they hunt lemmings and other prey.

Lemmings are mouselike rodents. In summer thousands and thousands of lemmings roam the land. In winter they spend their time in warm homes called burrows. Lemmings are important to the arctic food chain. They are food for predators such as weasels and foxes.

This giant musk ox wears a doubly thick coat. Its black outer layer protects the musk ox from wind and water. The light-colored inner layer keeps him warm. Meanwhile, in a snug nest below the frosty surface, a ground squirrel hibernates. It will sleep here all winter with almost no food or water.

Mother polar bears usually make cozy dens for themselves and their cubs. But even outside in the fiercest storms, their thick fur protects them from the ice and cold.

Finally, winter comes to an end and spring begins. The days are longer now, and the weather warms. Because the melting snow cannot drain through the frozen permafrost, the top layer of soil becomes soft and mushy. But ground like this is perfect for little bearberry and poppy plants to grow.

Lichens, too, come out. They cover the rocks and ground in shades of red, green, and yellow.

Lichen is actually made up of two kinds of living things. One is a type of algae, like the fuzzy green plants that grow on the glass of a fish tank. The other is a fungus, like a mushroom. The fungus holds up the algae, and the algae makes food for the fungus.

Now spring turns to summer. Suddenly the tundra bursts with life.

Many animals return from places farther south. Herds of caribou come back from their winter homes. Close behind are the arctic wolves that hunt them all year long.

Caribou are one of the great migrating animals of North America. Each year, great herds go back and forth between their summer home on the tundra and their winter home near the forests. Many caribou travel as much as 2,700 miles (4,340 kilometers) in a single year.

Birds are on the move, too. The western sandpipers fly
back from faraway Mexico. Swans, arctic terns, and
other birds return as well.

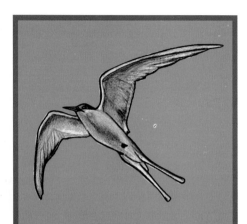

Each year the arctic
tern flies from the
tundra to the
Antarctic—and
back. It is a journey
of over 22,000 miles
(35,200 kilometers)
and is the longest
flight in the whole
bird kingdom.

By July, the temperature rises to nearly 60° F (16° C). Now the sun almost never sets, and the tundra becomes the land of the midnight sun.

In the warm summer air, insects swarm over the damp ground. Flowers brighten what had only weeks ago been a frozen desert. Birds and animals are everywhere. Many, like these ptarmigans, take on a brown color to help them hide in the summer grass.

Curious grizzly bears wander along, searching for juicy berries and roots. Even musk oxen change their coats. Shedding all that fur keeps these shaggy creatures comfortable during the summer.

Caribou graze contentedly on grass and plants. Above them, falcons soar and dive, on the lookout for prey. They hunt ptarmigans, lemmings, squirrels, and rabbits—always plentiful during the summer.

In no time at all, the arctic summer comes to an end. Quickly, the days grow shorter. Cold winds start to blow across the land, and plants give one final burst of color.

Again it is time for the birds, caribou, and many other animals to move on. As always, they are drawn by a mysterious power that makes them come and go with the changing seasons.

One by one, the animals that stay behind get ready for winter. Ground squirrels gather food and dig deep, cozy nests.

Among others, foxes and ptarmigans start to exchange their brown summer coats for thick white ones. Most of the insects die, but a few ready their bodies for the freezing cold.

Very swiftly, winter settles over the land. Once more, the arctic animals must brave the sunless days and bone-chilling cold . . . while the tundra waits for spring to return, many months away.

Walrus, Page 5:
One walrus will come to the rescue of another walrus if necessary. The first walrus will try to push the injured walrus off the ice and into the safety of the water.

Weasel, Page 15:
A weasel's white winter fur is called ermine. It has long been prized for its warmth and beauty. Weasels are slender enough to chase voles and lemmings down into their holes.

Wolf, Page 6:
Wolves live in family groups called packs. Scientists believe that wolves remain together because they share strong affectionate feelings.

Bearberry Plants, Page 18:
Trees and large bushes need deep roots to survive. But almost none of these can force their roots into the permafrost. That is why few trees exist on the tundra while this bearberry does very well.

Arctic Fox, Page 15:
A fox may bring back several lemmings to the family den. It will carry them in its mouth all at once. Or it may bring back goose eggs, one at a time, never breaking any.

Sandpiper, Page 22:
Sandpipers build their nests north of the arctic circle. They are small birds with long, sensitive bills. Many spend the winter months on warm southern seashores.

This Habitat

Ptarmigan, Page 23:
Feathers cover the feet, toes, and tail of a ptarmigan. The feathers help the ptarmigan stay warm and walk on top of the snow.

Falcon, Page 25:
Falcons are the fastest divers in the bird kingdom. They can swoop down on prey at speeds of up to 180 miles (290 kilometers) per hour.

Grizzly Bear, Page 24:
Grizzly cubs are born while the mother is asleep in her winter den. The newborn cubs weigh less than three pounds each (1.35 kilograms). Adult grizzlies weigh at least 600 pounds (270 kilograms).

Ground Squirrel, Page 27:
The Eskimo name for the arctic ground squirrel is the sik-sik. Arctic ground squirrels shift from patches of sun to shady spots to warm up and cool off during the summer.

Musk Ox, Page 24:
To protect their young, adult musk oxen form a circle facing outward, with their babies in the middle. This shoulder-to-shoulder defense keeps baby musk oxen safe from wolves.

Polar Bear, Page 29:
Polar bears have pads of fur on the soles of their feet. The fur helps keep the bears' feet warm and also helps them walk on the ice.